sun

rubber ring

girl

boy

swimming costume

swimming trunks

hat

wave

sea

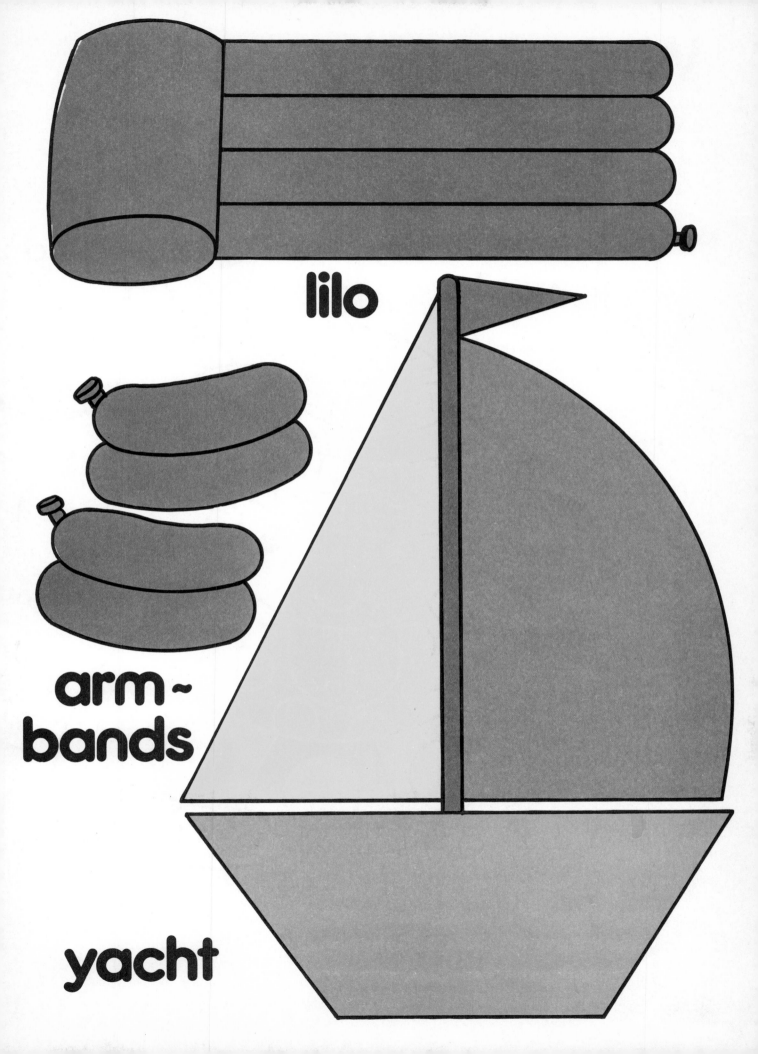

lilo

arm~
bands

yacht

What can you see?

ice cream

seagull

beach

sand

donkey

ice cream van

breakwater

saddle

pier

What can you see?

crab

shrimp

net

lighthouse

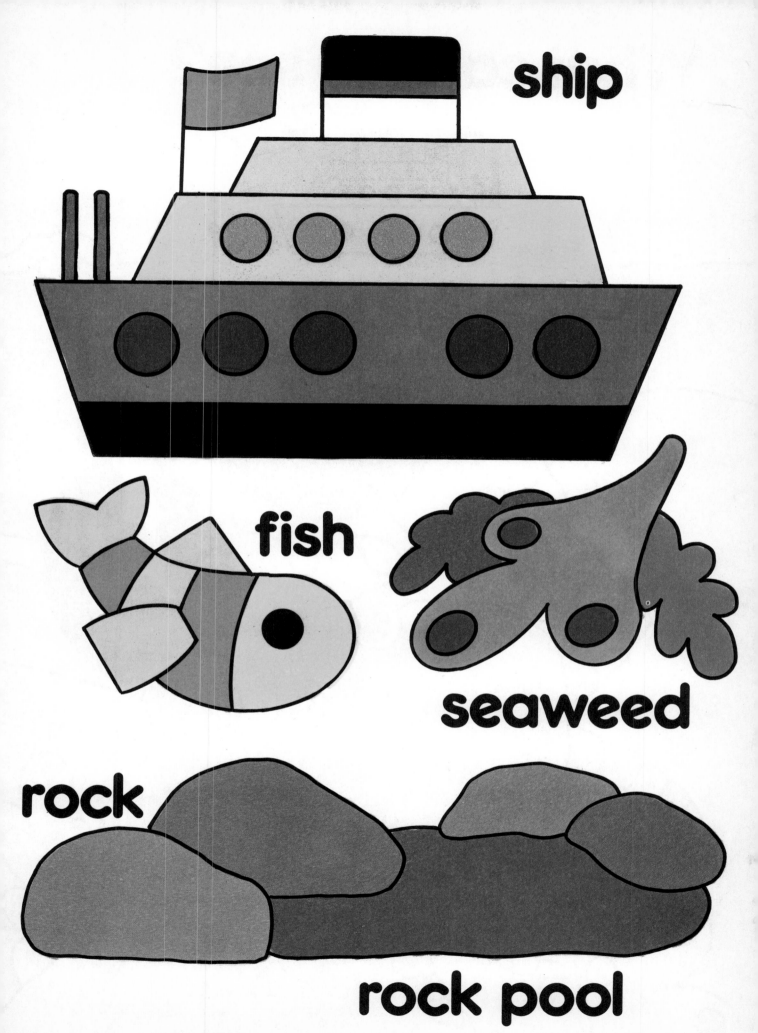

ship

fish

seaweed

rock

rock pool

What can you see?

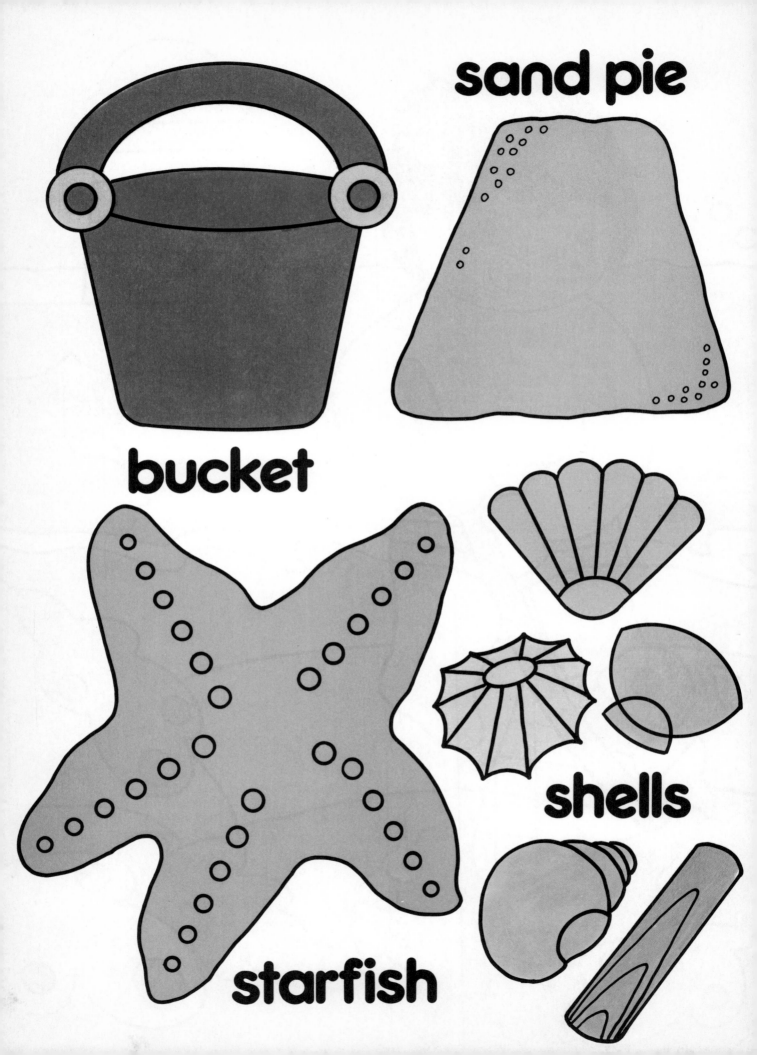

sand pie

bucket

shells

starfish

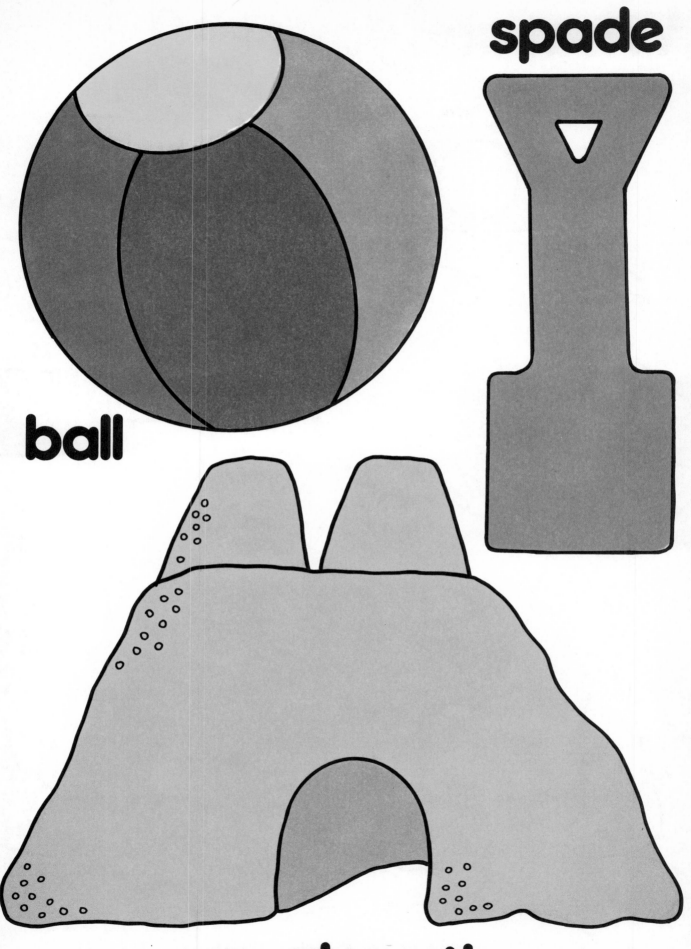

ball

spade

sand castle

What can you see?

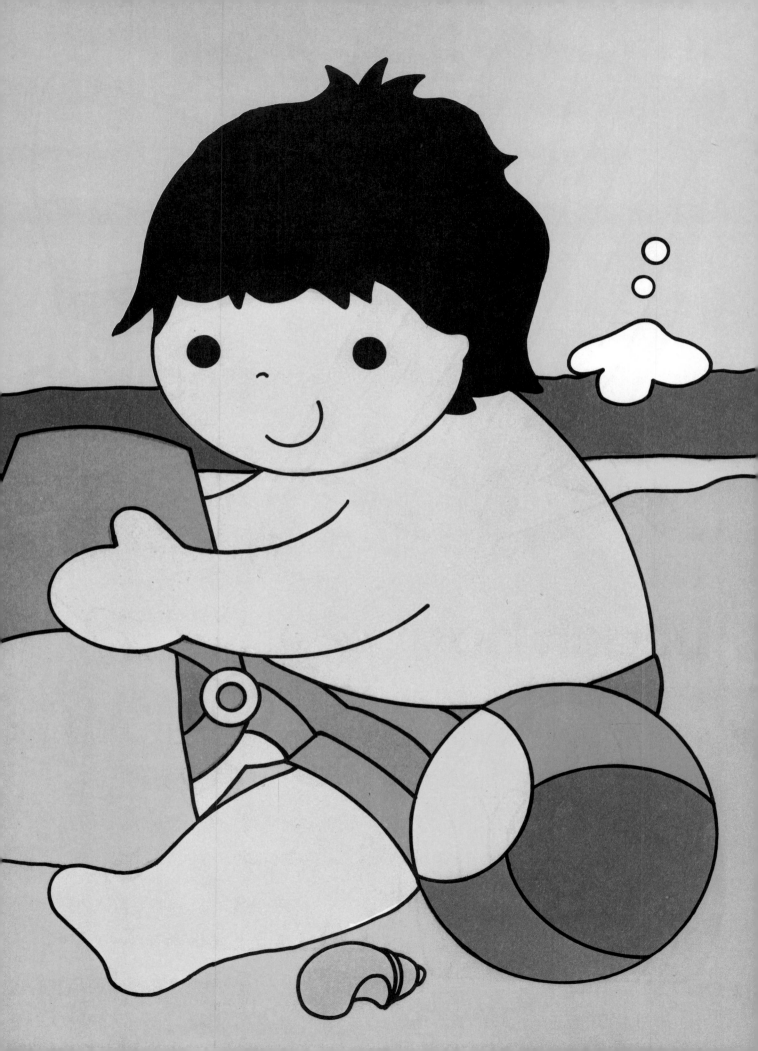

deck chair

sandwich

beach bag

towel

sunshade

orange

sunglasses

picnic hamper

What can you see?